HOW TO WIN THE PROPERTY WAR IN YOUR BANKRUPTCY

Winning at Law

JOHN ELLSWORTH, ESQ.

American Legal Publishers

How To Win the Property War

Part I

$$1$$

Bankruptcy and Divorce

Navigating Financial Complexities in Divorce: Bankruptcy, Debt, and Beyond

Introduction

Divorce is not just an emotional journey but also a complex financial negotiation. Among the myriad issues that couples face during a divorce, dealing with shared debts and considering bankruptcy are critical. Understanding the timing and impact of these financial decisions is crucial for both parties.

Financial Implications of Divorce

Divorce often involves splitting assets and debts. Shared debts can include mortgages, car loans, credit card debts, and in some cases, back taxes. How these are divided can significantly impact each individual's financial situation post-divorce.

Bankruptcy and Divorce: Timing Matters

Filing for Bankruptcy Before Divorce:

• **Pros:** Filing jointly for bankruptcy before divorce can simplify debt issues in the divorce proceedings. It can potentially discharge shared debts, making the financial aspects of the divorce simpler.

• **Cons:** However, discharging debts before divorce might leave more assets to be divided in the divorce settlement. This could potentially mean higher alimony or child support payments, as the paying spouse may have a higher disposable income.

Filing for Bankruptcy After Divorce:

• **Pros:** Waiting to file for bankruptcy until after the divorce can protect the individual who is more financially stable from the other's bankruptcy. This might be a strategic choice if there's a significant imbalance in the financial situations of the divorcing parties.

• **Cons:** The downside is the complexity it adds to the divorce process, as the division of debt becomes more complicated.

Ethical Considerations

Using bankruptcy as a strategic tool in divorce, particularly as a means to shift financial burdens unfairly onto a former spouse, raises serious ethical concerns. It's essential to approach these matters with fairness and integrity. The goal should be to reach an equitable solution that considers the well-being of all parties involved, including children.

Child Support and Alimony

Child support and alimony are calculated based on income and the financial needs of the children and ex-spouse. It's important to remember that these are legal obligations. Manipulating one's financial situation to reduce these obligations can have legal repercussions and long-term impacts on the children's welfare.

The Emotional and Financial Toll of Divorce

Divorce is not just a legal process; it's an emotional one that can have lasting financial impacts. Both parties should focus on making decisions that lead to financial stability and fairness. This might involve working with financial planners, lawyers, and counselors.

Conclusion

Navigating the intersection of divorce, bankruptcy, and debt requires a thorough understanding of the legal implications and a commitment to ethical decision-making. The focus should be on achieving a fair outcome that respects the financial and emotional well-being of all parties involved. Remember, the decisions made during a divorce can have lasting impacts, and it's important to approach them with care and consideration.

· · ·

THIS ARTICLE PROVIDES a balanced view of the complexities involved in managing finances during a divorce, emphasizing the need for ethical decision-making and considering the long-term impacts of these decisions.

Can I File Chapter 7 or 13 at My Choice?

When deciding to file for bankruptcy in the United States, you don't always have the choice between Chapter 7 and Chapter 13; there are specific qualifying criteria for each.

Means Test for Chapter 7:

• The means test determines if your income is low enough to file for Chapter 7 bankruptcy.

• It compares your average monthly income for the six months before your bankruptcy against the median income for a similar household in your state.

• If your income is below the median, you can file for Chapter 7.

• If your income is above the median, you might still qualify based on a calculation of your disposable income and unsecured debts.

Qualifications for Chapter 13:

• Chapter 13 is typically for individuals who have a regular income and can pay back a portion of their debts through a repayment plan.

• There are debt limits for Chapter 13: unsecured debts must be less than $419,275 and secured debts less than $1,257,850 (as of April 2021; these amounts adjust periodically).

• If your debt exceeds these limits, you cannot file for Chapter 13.

Other Considerations:

• Previous Bankruptcies: Your eligibility for Chapter 7 or 13 can also depend on any previous bankruptcies you've filed.

• Non-exempt Assets: If you have substantial non-exempt assets you wish to keep, Chapter 13 may be more suitable.

• Personal Goals: Your personal financial goals and circumstances also play a role in choosing the type of bankruptcy.

Each type of bankruptcy has different advantages, requirements, and consequences. It's advisable to consult with a bankruptcy attorney to understand which chapter is most suitable for your specific situation.

Part II

Pros and Cons of Filing for Bankruptcy

Advantages of Filing for Bankruptcy:

Stop Creditor Harassment: Filing for bankruptcy gives you relief from creditors. While your case is ongoing, they can't collect debts or seize assets like your home or car. If debts are wiped out in bankruptcy, collectors can't chase you for them anymore.

Protect Your Future Income: Money you earn after filing for bankruptcy is usually safe from old debts that are erased in the process. But, be aware that new debts, like child support, might still affect your future income.

Emotional Relief: Dealing with debt is stressful. Bankruptcy can give you a fresh start, reducing stress and improving your overall well-being.

Keep Essential Assets: You won't lose everything in bankruptcy. Laws allow you to keep key assets like your home, car, clothes, and some other valuables, within certain dollar limits.

Federal Bankruptcy Exemption Limits:
- Home: $27,900
- Car: $4,450
- Household Goods: $14,875 total, $700 per item
- Jewelry: $1,875
- Wild Card (any property): $1,475

- Wild Card (unused home exemption): $13,950
- Work Tools: $2,800
- Personal Injury Claims: $27,900
- Life Insurance: $14,875
- Education Savings: $7,575
- Retirement Accounts: Over $1.5 million

(These amounts can vary by state and are doubled for married couples.)

Disadvantages of Filing for Bankruptcy:

Credit Score Impact: Bankruptcy can significantly harm your credit score for up to 10 years. However, you can start rebuilding your credit immediately, for example, by using a secured credit card.

Costs: Filing for bankruptcy isn't free. It costs $313 for Chapter 13 and $338 for Chapter 7, plus lawyer fees.

Loss of Luxury Items: Bankruptcy might force you to sell non-essential, luxury items. In Chapter 13, their value influences your repayment plan.

Future Borrowing Challenges: It's harder to get new loans with a bankruptcy on your record. After a Chapter 7 filing, you might need to wait 2-4 years before applying for a mortgage.

Chapters of Bankruptcy

Bankruptcies are named after their chapter in the federal bankruptcy law. Thus you have *Chapter 7*, *Chapter 11*, *Chapter 12*, *Chapter 13*.

Filing bankruptcy can help a person by discarding debt or making a plan to repay debts. A bankruptcy case normally begins when the debtor files a petition with the bankruptcy court. A petition may be filed by an individual, by spouses together, or by a corporation or other entity.

All bankruptcy cases are handled in federal courts under rules outlined in the U.S. Bankruptcy Code.

There are different types of bankruptcies, which are usually referred to by their chapter in the U.S. Bankruptcy Code.

• Individuals may file <u>Chapter 7</u> or <u>Chapter 13</u> bankruptcy, depending on the specifics of their situation.

• Municipalities—cities, towns, villages, taxing districts, municipal utilities, and school districts may file under <u>Chapter 9</u> to reorganize.

• Businesses may file bankruptcy under <u>Chapter 7</u> to liquidate or <u>Chapter 11</u> to reorganize.

• <u>Chapter 12</u> provides debt relief to family farmers and fishermen.

• Bankruptcy filings that involve parties from more than one country are filed under <u>Chapter 15</u>.

<u>Bankruptcy Basics</u> provides detailed information about filing.

Seeking the advice of a qualified lawyer is strongly recommended because bankruptcy has long-term financial and legal consequences. Individuals can file bankruptcy without a lawyer, which is called filing pro se. <u>Learn more</u>.

Use the forms that are numbered in the 100 series to file bankruptcy for individuals or married couples. Use the forms that are numbered in the 200 series if you are preparing a bankruptcy on behalf of a non-individual, such as a corporation, partnership, or limited liability company (LLC). Sole proprietors must use the forms that are numbered in the 100 series.

Finding a Lawyer, Including Free Legal Services

If you need help finding a bankruptcy lawyer, the resources below may help. If you are unable to afford an attorney, you may qualify for free legal services.

- <u>American Bar Association's Legal Help website</u><u>(link is external)</u>
- <u>Legal Services Corporation</u>

Lawyer or DIY?

Hiring a Lawyer for Bankruptcy:

• **Complex Cases:** If you have a complicated financial situation, including owning substantial assets, running a business, or facing potential legal actions from creditors, a lawyer can help navigate these complexities.

• **Legal Expertise:** Bankruptcy lawyers are well-versed in state and federal laws that will affect your case, including which exemptions can protect your assets and how to handle the means test for Chapter 7.

• **Representation:** An attorney can represent you in court and in dealings with creditors, reducing the stress and burden of the legal process.

DIY Bankruptcy:

• **Simple Cases:** If your case is straightforward, with few assets and clear-cut debts, you might consider a DIY approach, especially if you cannot afford an attorney.

• **Educational Resources:** There are resources available, such as books, online guides, and court-provided information, that can help you understand the process.

• **Cost Savings:** The primary advantage of a DIY bankruptcy is avoiding legal fees, which can be significant.

However, it's important to note that bankruptcy can have long-lasting financial and legal consequences. Mistakes in the filing process can result in the dismissal of your case, the forfeiture of non-exempt assets, or even allegations of bankruptcy fraud. Given the potential risks, many people find that hiring a lawyer is a prudent investment to ensure their rights are protected and to increase the likelihood of a successful outcome.

Whether you choose to hire a lawyer or proceed on your own, make sure you are well-informed about the requirements and risks associated with filing for bankruptcy.

Filing Without a Lawyer

Filing Without an Attorney

Individuals can file bankruptcy without an attorney, which is called filing pro se. However, seeking the advice of a qualified attorney is strongly recommended because bankruptcy has long-term financial and legal outcomes.

Filing personal bankruptcy under Chapter 7 or Chapter 13 takes careful preparation and understanding of legal issues. Misunderstandings of the law or making mistakes in the process can affect your rights. Court employees and bankruptcy judges are prohibited by law from offering legal advice.

The following is a list of ways your lawyer can help you with your case.

- Advise you on whether to file a bankruptcy petition.
- Advise you under which chapter to file.
- Advise you on whether your debts can be discharged.
- Advise you on whether or not you will be able to keep your home, car, or other property after you file.
- Advise you of the tax consequences of filing.
- Advise you on whether you should continue to pay creditors.
- Explain bankruptcy law and procedures to you.
- Help you complete and file forms.

• Assist you with most aspects of your bankruptcy case.

Pro se litigants are expected to follow the rules and procedures in federal courts and should be familiar with the <u>United States Bankruptcy Code</u>

(<u>link is external</u>)

,and the <u>Federal Rules of Bankruptcy Procedure</u>

(<u>link is external</u>)

AND THE LOCAL rules of the court in which the case is filed. Local rules, along with other useful information, are posted on the court's website and are available at the local court's intake counter. Court employees and bankruptcy judges are prohibited by law from offering legal advice.

<u>Bankruptcy Forms</u> are available to the public free of charge.

• Use the forms that are numbered in the 100 series to file bankruptcy for individuals or married couples.

• Use the forms that are numbered in the 200 series if you are preparing a bankruptcy on behalf of a nonindividual, such as a corporation, partnership, or limited liability company (LLC).

• Sole proprietors must use the forms that are numbered in the 100 series.

Many courts require local forms. You should check your court's website before filing any documents.

Non-attorney Petition Preparers

If you file bankruptcy pro se, you may be offered services by non-attorney petition preparers. By law, preparers can only enter information into forms. They are prohibited from providing legal advice, explaining answers to legal questions, or assisting you in bankruptcy court. A petition preparer must sign all documents they prepare for you; print their name, address and social security on the documents; and provide you with a copy of all documents. They cannot sign documents on your behalf or receive payment for court fees.

Finding a Lawyer, Including Free Legal Services

If you need help finding a bankruptcy lawyer, the resources below may help. If you are unable to afford an attorney, you may qualify for free legal services.

- <u>American Bar Association's Legal Help</u>(link is external).
- <u>Legal Services Corporation</u>

Credit Counseling - Mandatory

Credit Counseling and Debtor Education Courses

All individual bankruptcy filers are required to complete pre-bankruptcy credit counseling and pre-discharge debtor education. These may not be provided at the same time. Credit counseling must take place before you file for bankruptcy; debtor education must take place after you file.

Certificate of completion for both credit counseling and debtor education are required but before the filer's debts can be discharged. Only credit counseling organizations and debtor education course providers that have been approved by the <u>U.S. Trustee Program</u> may issue these certificates. Find an approved <u>credit counseling agency</u> or <u>debtor education provider</u>.

Filers in Alabama and North Carolina

By law, the U.S. Trustee Program does not operate in Alabama and North Carolina; in these states, <u>Bankruptcy Administrators</u> approve pre-bankruptcy credit counseling organizations and pre-discharge debtor education course providers. The following is a list of Bankruptcy Administrator approved providers in Alabama and North Carolina.

Credit Counseling

Alabama Northern
Alabama Middle
Alabama Southern
North Carolina Eastern
North Carolina Middle
North Carolina Western
Debtor Education
Alabama Northern
Alabama Middle
Alabama Southern
North Carolina Eastern
North Carolina Middle
North Carolina Western
Filers in all other states and territories

Certificate of completion for both credit counseling and debtor education are required but before the filer's debts can be discharged. Only credit counseling organizations and debtor education course providers that have been approved by the U.S. Trustee Program may issue these certificates for filers in all states and territories except for Alabama and North Carolina. Find an approved credit counseling agency or debtor education provider.

Approval Process for Credit Counseling and Debtor Education Courses

In Alabama and North Carolina, the bankruptcy administrator approves credit counseling and debtor education providers. Lists of approved providers for the six judicial districts in Alabama and North Carolina are maintained by the bankruptcy administrator for that district or bankruptcy court.

An entity seeking to become an authorized credit counseling or debtor education provider in Alabama or North Carolina must go through an application process administered by the bankruptcy administrator for that district.

The United States Bankruptcy Administrator Program, a bankruptcy estate administration program established by the federal judiciary, presently serves only the six federal judicial districts in the States of Alabama and North Carolina.

The bankruptcy administrator program is separate from the U.S. trustee program in the Department of Justice, and information on the application process for credit counseling agencies and debtor education course providers in any jurisdictions other than Alabama and North Carolina can be found on the Department of Justice web site at www.usdoj.gov/ust.

Part III

8

Introduction to Bankruptcy Types

Strategic Use of Chapter 7 and Chapter 13 Bankruptcy

For many facing financial hardship, bankruptcy offers a path to relief and recovery. However, the choice between Chapter 7 and Chapter 13 is not merely a matter of preference but one of strategic financial planning. Understanding when and why to choose one over the other can significantly impact the outcome of your bankruptcy filing.

Chapter 7: Liquidation for a Fresh Start

Chapter 7 bankruptcy is a liquidation process that can quickly discharge most unsecured debts, such as credit card debt and medical bills. It's generally chosen by those with limited income and few assets.

When to Choose Chapter 7:

• **Minimal Assets:** If you have little to no non-exempt property, Chapter 7 can provide a clean slate without the risk of losing substantial assets.

• **Limited Income:** Passing the means test — which indicates your income is below the state median for your household size — is a prerequisite.

• **Immediate Relief Needed:** If you need to eliminate overwhelming debt swiftly due to pending lawsuits, wage garnishments, or imminent foreclosures, Chapter 7 offers a quicker resolution.

Chapter 13: Reorganization to Retain Assets

Chapter 13 bankruptcy is about reorganizing debt. Debtors with regular income develop a plan to repay all or part of their debts over a three to five-year period.

When to Choose Chapter 13:

• **Home Equity:** If you have significant equity in your home that exceeds state exemptions, Chapter 13 can protect your home from being sold to satisfy debts.

• **Regular Income:** A consistent income is required to meet the repayment plan obligations.

• **Catching Up on Payments:** If you're behind on a mortgage or car loan, Chapter 13 can halt foreclosure and repossession efforts, giving you time to catch up.

• **Non-Dischargeable Debts:** Certain tax obligations and domestic support arrears can be managed through a Chapter 13 repayment plan.

Using Both Chapters Strategically

Sometimes, individuals can strategically use both chapters in what is informally known as a "Chapter 20" bankruptcy — filing for Chapter 13 after a Chapter 7 discharge.

When to Consider a "Chapter 20" Strategy:

• **Lien Stripping:** If a first mortgage is secured by the full value of the home, second and third mortgages can become unsecured debts in a subsequent Chapter 13, potentially allowing for their discharge.

• **Managing Non-Dischargeable Debts:** If Chapter 7 doesn't eliminate all debts, a follow-up Chapter 13 can help manage the remaining obligations.

• **Additional Time:** If you received a Chapter 7 discharge but still need time to catch up on certain debts without creditor harassment, filing for Chapter 13 can provide that breathing room.

Factors Influencing the Decision

Several factors can influence the decision to file under one chapter or another, including:

• **Asset Types and Values:** Exemptions under Chapter 7 protect certain assets, but if your assets exceed these exemptions, Chapter 13 may be preferable.

• **Income Level:** Your income level can disqualify you from Chapter 7 but could be ideal for a Chapter 13 repayment plan.

• **Long-Term Goals:** If keeping your home is a priority, Chapter 13 is often the better route. Conversely, if you seek the quickest way to debt relief and have no significant assets, Chapter 7 may be more appropriate.

Conclusion

Choosing between Chapter 7 and Chapter 13 bankruptcy should be a calculated decision based on an individual's financial situation, goals, and the types of debt they carry. Each chapter offers unique protections and serves different needs. Sometimes, employing both chapters consecutively provides the best solution to complex financial problems.

It is critical to consult with a bankruptcy attorney to explore your options thoroughly. A legal professional can provide tailored advice and develop a strategic plan that aligns with your financial objectives and offers the most beneficial outcome.

THIS CHAPTER IS for informational purposes and should not substitute for professional legal advice. Bankruptcy laws are complex, and strategies should be discussed with a bankruptcy lawyer who can offer guidance specific to your circumstances.

9

Exemptions

The purpose of exemptions is to help you keep certain property.

Use Exemptions to Protect Property

Both federal and state laws offer bankruptcy exemptions that allow you to keep certain property up to a certain value.

• **Homestead Exemption:** Protects equity in your primary residence.

• **Vehicle Exemption:** May cover your car up to a certain value.

• **Personal Property Exemptions:** Includes clothing, furniture, and other household goods.

• **Wildcard Exemptions:** Can be applied to the property of your choice.

It's important to consult with a bankruptcy attorney to determine which exemptions you can use and how they apply in your state.

Timing

Consider the Timing of Your Bankruptcy

Timing can influence the amount of property you can exempt. For instance, if you're expecting a significant change in income or assets, filing before such changes can be beneficial.

Reaffirmation

Choosing property to keep paying for so you get to keep it. This is no magician's magic in the bankruptcy code. It's just a formal way of telling the court and the people you owe that here is a piece of property that means so much to you, paying and keeping is your choice.

Reaffirm Secured Debts

In some cases, you can sign a reaffirmation agreement with a lender for secured debts like a car loan or mortgage. This agreement excludes those debts from bankruptcy, allowing you to keep the collateral as long as you continue to make payments.

Change CharacterizationConvert Non-Exempt Assets into Exempt Assets

Convert Non-Exempt Assets into Exempt Assets

Before filing, you might convert non-exempt assets into exempt ones. For example, using non-exempt cash to pay down the mortgage on your home could protect it under a homestead exemption.

Is Chapter 13 a Better Choice
for You?

Chapter 13 vs. Chapter 7: When Chapter 13 is the Better Choice

Filing for bankruptcy is a decision that can significantly affect your financial future. Understanding the differences between Chapter 13 and Chapter 7 bankruptcy is essential in making an informed choice. Chapter 13 is often the better option under several circumstances.

Retaining Ownership of Assets

Chapter 13: Allows debtors to keep their property and pay debts over time. It's ideal for those with a steady income who can stick to a repayment plan but wish to avoid liquidation of their assets.

Chapter 7: Involves the liquidation of non-exempt assets to pay off creditors. If you have considerable equity in your home or other assets that are not covered by exemptions, Chapter 7 could result in losing those assets.

Handling Secured Debts

Chapter 13: If you are behind on your mortgage or car payments, Chapter 13 bankruptcy can help you catch up on arrears over the life of the repayment plan, thus avoiding foreclosure or repossession.

Chapter 7: Does not provide a way to catch up on missed

payments for secured debts. It may only temporarily delay foreclosure or repossession.

Dealing with Non-Dischargeable Debts

Chapter 13: Certain debts that are not dischargeable in Chapter 7, like some taxes or missed child support payments, can be included in the Chapter 13 repayment plan, allowing you to pay them off over time without accruing additional penalties or interest.

Chapter 7: Does not offer a structured plan to handle non-dischargeable debts; you remain fully responsible for these debts after other debts have been discharged.

Modifying Secured Debt

Chapter 13: Offers the possibility to "cram down" certain secured debts — reducing the debt to the value of the asset. This can be beneficial for underwater assets, such as a car loan where the balance exceeds the value of the car.

Chapter 7: There is no opportunity to cram down secured debts. You either continue to pay the loan as agreed, surrender the property, or, in some cases, reaffirm the debt.

Protecting Co-Debtors

Chapter 13: The co-debtor stay in Chapter 13 protects co-signers on consumer debts while the repayment plan is in effect.

Chapter 7: Does not provide such protection for co-signers, who may then be pursued by creditors for the debt if you discharge your obligation in bankruptcy.

Overcoming the Means Test

Chapter 13: If your income is too high to qualify for Chapter 7 bankruptcy under the means test, Chapter 13 may be your only option. It allows those with higher incomes to reorganize their debts and still receive bankruptcy protection.

Chapter 7: You must pass the means test, which compares your income to the median income for your state. If you earn too much, you may be ineligible for Chapter 7.

Addressing Student Loans

Chapter 13: While typically not dischargeable, student loans can be included in your repayment plan, potentially lowering your payments during the plan period.

Chapter 7: Offers no specific relief for student loans outside of rare cases where undue hardship is proven.

Advantages of Flexibility

Chapter 13: Offers flexibility during the plan. Debtors can sometimes adjust their payments due to changes in their financial situation or even convert their case to a Chapter 7 if necessary.

Chapter 7: Offers less flexibility once the bankruptcy process has begun.

In conclusion, Chapter 13 bankruptcy often serves as the better option for those who have significant equity in their assets, are facing foreclosure or repossession, have a regular income that exceeds the Chapter 7 means test, or have specific types of debt that are better managed under a repayment plan. It is a powerful tool for debt reorganization, providing a pathway to financial recovery while maintaining ownership of your valued assets.

Choosing the right type of bankruptcy is a pivotal decision that should be made with careful consideration and professional guidance. An experienced bankruptcy attorney can assess your financial situation and help you understand which chapter would be most beneficial for you.

THE ABOVE CHAPTER is intended to provide a general overview and should not be taken as legal advice. Laws and personal circumstances vary widely, so individuals should consult a licensed attorney for advice on their specific situation.

Do I Need a Lawyer?

You need a lawyer. Bankruptcy today is extremely complex and there are literally hundreds of gotchas that can suddenly take away a car you need for work and allow a creditor make you keep paying their bill or pay taxes you no longer owe.

Here is the key resource for finding a good lawyer: the National Association of Consumer Bankruptcy Attorneys (NACBA) can provide resources or references to reputable bankruptcy paper preparers.

And a chapter 13 would be impossible for a lay person to accomplish without losing everything.

Most lawyers have payment plans. Most bankruptcy districts have free bankruptcy clinics for citizens in need.

PART II

Bankruptcy Process

Who Does What In My Bankruptcy?

In a Chapter 13 bankruptcy, several key participants each play a distinct role in the process. Here's an overview of these participants and their respective roles:

The Debtor

The debtor is the individual (or married couple) filing for Chapter 13 bankruptcy. The debtor's role is to provide complete and accurate information about their finances, including assets, liabilities, income, and expenses. They must also attend counseling sessions, file the necessary paperwork, adhere to the repayment plan, and attend the 341 meeting of creditors.

The Trustee

The trustee in a Chapter 13 bankruptcy acts as an intermediary between the debtor and the creditors. The trustee's role includes:

• **Reviewing the Case:** The trustee examines the debtor's petition and financial information to ensure accuracy and to assess the feasibility of the proposed repayment plan.

• **Administering the Repayment Plan:** The trustee collects payments from the debtor and distributes them to creditors in accordance with the plan.

• **Overseeing Compliance:** The trustee monitors the debtor's compliance with the repayment plan and can bring issues to the court's attention if the debtor fails to make payments or meet other requirements.

The Bankruptcy Judge

The bankruptcy judge presides over the court and has the authority to make legal decisions regarding the bankruptcy. The judge's role includes:

• **Confirmation of the Repayment Plan:** The judge evaluates and either confirms or denies the debtor's repayment plan based on its fairness and compliance with bankruptcy laws.

• **Resolution of Disputes:** The judge resolves disputes between the debtor, the trustee, and creditors.

• **Legal Oversight:** The judge oversees the legal proceedings and ensures the bankruptcy process is carried out according to the law.

The Debtor's Attorney

The debtor's attorney (if they choose to hire one) represents the debtor throughout the bankruptcy. The attorney's role includes:

• **Legal Advice:** Providing legal advice to the debtor on bankruptcy laws and the implications of filing.

• **Preparation of Documents:** Preparing and filing the necessary documents with the bankruptcy court.

• **Representation:** Representing the debtor in court and in dealings with the trustee and creditors.

• **Advocacy:** Advocating on behalf of the debtor, particularly when legal issues or disputes arise.

The Creditors

Creditors are the entities to whom the debtor owes money. In Chapter 13 bankruptcy, creditors' roles include:

• **Filing Proofs of Claim:** Submitting proofs of claim to the court to establish the legitimacy and amount of their claims.

• **Participating in Meetings:** Attending the 341 meeting of creditors to question the debtor about their financial situation and the proposed repayment plan.

• **Objecting to the Plan:** Creditors can object to the repayment plan if they believe it doesn't comply with bankruptcy laws or if they will receive less than what they would under a Chapter 7 liquidation.

Creditors' Attorneys

Attorneys representing the creditors play a role similar to that of the debtor's attorney but with a focus on protecting the creditors' interests. Their role includes:

• **Legal Representation:** Representing the creditor in the bankruptcy process.

• **Filing Objections:** Filing objections to the repayment plan or to the dischargeability of certain debts.

• **Negotiation:** Engaging in negotiations with the debtor's attorney or trustee to protect the creditor's claim.

Each participant in a Chapter 13 bankruptcy has a role that contributes to the fair and orderly progression of the bankruptcy case. Their interactions and the balance of their interests are structured by bankruptcy law to ensure that the debtor can manage their debts while creditors receive as much payment as possible within the debtor's financial constraints.

Chronology (Timing)

Bankruptcy proceedings can vary significantly depending on whether it's a Chapter 7 or Chapter 13 case. Here's a comparative chronology for both:

Chapter 7 Bankruptcy (Liquidation)

Filing the Petition: The debtor files a petition with the bankruptcy court. This includes schedules of assets and liabilities, a statement of financial affairs, and more.

Automatic Stay: An automatic stay is immediately enacted, stopping most collection actions against the debtor or their property.

Meeting of Creditors: Around 20-40 days after filing, a meeting of creditors is held, where the debtor is questioned under oath.

Trustee Sells Assets: A trustee sells the debtor's non-exempt assets to pay creditors.

Debt Discharge: Remaining unsecured debts are discharged, typically within 4-6 months of filing.

Chapter 13 Bankruptcy (Reorganization)

Filing the Petition: Similar to Chapter 7, the debtor files a petition along with detailed financial documentation.

Automatic Stay: The automatic stay also applies in Chapter 13, halting most collection efforts.

Meeting of Creditors: This is similar to Chapter 7, occurring within 20-40 days of filing.

Repayment Plan: The debtor proposes a repayment plan to make installments to creditors over three to five years. This plan must be submitted with the petition or within 14 days after the petition is filed.

Confirmation Hearing: The bankruptcy judge holds a hearing to decide whether to approve the plan.

Making Payments: The debtor begins making payments according to the plan.

Debt Discharge: Upon completion of all plan payments, most remaining debts are discharged.

Key Differences

• **Asset Liquidation:** Chapter 7 involves liquidating non-exempt assets, while Chapter 13 focuses on a repayment plan.

• **Time Frame:** Chapter 7 is generally quicker (4-6 months) compared to Chapter 13 (3-5 years).

• **Debt Limits:** Chapter 13 has debt limits, whereas Chapter 7 does not.

• **Property Retention:** In Chapter 13, debtors can keep their property but must make payments according to the plan. In Chapter 7, non-exempt property might be sold.

Both processes are complex and have significant financial and legal implications. Most lawyers, including myself, always recommend hiring a lawyer.

PART III

Bankruptcy Crimes

17

Bankruptcy Crimes

Bankruptcy crimes are federal offenses that occur in the context of bankruptcy proceedings. These crimes are typically committed with the intent to deceive the bankruptcy court, creditors, and other parties involved in the bankruptcy process. Here are some of the most common bankruptcy crimes, how they occur, the intent behind them, their discovery, investigation, prosecution, and the potential penalties.

Common Bankruptcy Crimes

Bankruptcy Fraud: Concealing assets to avoid having to forfeit them; intentionally filing false or incomplete forms; filing multiple times using either personal identifiers or false information in different states.

Concealment of Assets: Not disclosing all assets or transferring them to friends or relatives before or after filing for bankruptcy.

False Statements: Making false statements under oath during bankruptcy proceedings or on bankruptcy paperwork.

Fraudulent Conveyance: Transferring property to another person or business with the intent to defraud creditors.

Bribery: Offering something of value to a trustee or bankruptcy official to influence their actions.

How and Why They Occur

• **Intent to Protect Assets**: Individuals may conceal assets or commit fraud to protect their property from liquidation or to obtain a discharge of debts without actually qualifying for it.

• **Financial Pressure**: In the face of overwhelming debt, individuals may make desperate, illegal choices to relieve their financial burdens.

• **Lack of Knowledge**: Some individuals commit bankruptcy crimes out of ignorance of the legal requirements and processes involved in bankruptcy.

Discovery of the Crime

Bankruptcy crimes are often discovered through:

• **Audits**: Random or targeted audits by the bankruptcy court or trustee can uncover discrepancies.

• **Creditor Claims**: Creditors may notice missing assets or inconsistencies in the debtor's paperwork and report them.

• **Whistleblowers**: Individuals who know the debtor might report suspicious activities.

• **Investigation of Financial Records**: Trustees and investigators will review financial records and may notice hidden assets or unusual transactions.

Investigation

Bankruptcy crimes are primarily investigated by:

• **The FBI**: As the principal investigative arm for federal crimes, the FBI has jurisdiction over bankruptcy fraud.

• **The U.S. Trustee Program**: Part of the Department of Justice, it oversees the administration of bankruptcy cases and can refer cases to the FBI.

• **IRS**: In cases where tax fraud is involved, the IRS may also participate in the investigation.

Prosecution

Bankruptcy crimes are prosecuted by:

• **The U.S. Attorney's Office**: Federal prosecutors in the U.S. Attorney's Office will prosecute bankruptcy crimes in federal court.

Penalties

Penalties for bankruptcy crimes can include:

• **Prison Time**: Sentences can range from a few years to up to 20 years for severe fraud.

- **Fines**: Substantial fines can be imposed, often in the tens or hundreds of thousands of dollars.
- **Restitution**: The court may order the offender to pay restitution to the victims of the crime.
- **Denial of Discharge**: The debtor's discharge can be denied, leaving them legally responsible for all debts.

The actual sentence will depend on the nature and severity of the crime, the value of the assets involved, the individual's criminal history, and other factors. The penalties are designed not only to punish the offender but also to deter others from attempting similar crimes. It's important to note that even an attempt to commit a bankruptcy crime, or a conspiracy to commit such a crime, is punishable under federal law.

YOU

the dangers of lying at your first creditors meeting, and what could happen to people who do not disclose all of their property, or Hwy lie about other things in their bankruptcy

The first meeting of creditors, also known as the 341 meeting, is a mandatory part of the bankruptcy process where debtors are required to answer questions about their finances and bankruptcy papers under oath. Lying at this meeting, or in any part of the bankruptcy process, can have serious consequences due to the following dangers:

Perjury

The most immediate risk of lying is the charge of perjury. Since the meeting of creditors is conducted under oath, any intentional falsehoods can result in perjury charges. Perjury is a federal crime and can lead to prison sentences, fines, or both.

Denial of Discharge

A debtor caught lying about their assets or finances can have their bankruptcy discharge denied. This means that the debtor would remain liable for all debts, despite having gone through the bankruptcy process.

Revocation of Discharge

If the dishonesty is discovered after the discharge has been granted, the court can revoke the discharge. This can occur if the fraud is discovered within one year after the discharge or sometimes even later.

Loss of Bankruptcy Exemptions

If a debtor is found to have lied about their assets, they may lose the right to claim certain exemptions. This could result in more of their property being available to creditors to satisfy debts.

Criminal Charges

In addition to perjury, a debtor who lies may face other criminal charges, such as bankruptcy fraud, which carries a potential sentence of up to five years in prison, fines, or both.

Civil Lawsuits

Apart from the bankruptcy proceeding itself, debtors who lie might also face civil lawsuits from creditors or trustees to recover concealed assets.

Investigation by the FBI

Bankruptcy fraud is a federal crime and is investigated by the FBI. If a debtor is suspected of lying or hiding assets, the case may be referred to the FBI for investigation. This can lead to a full-blown investigation into all aspects of the debtor's financial life.

Professional Consequences

For professionals who are held to a higher standard of ethics, such as lawyers or accountants, being caught lying in bankruptcy proceedings can lead to additional disciplinary actions by licensing boards or professional associations.

Personal and Social Consequences

Aside from legal consequences, individuals who lie in bankruptcy proceedings may also suffer personal and social repercussions. The public nature of bankruptcy cases can result in a loss of reputation and trustworthiness.

How Lies are Discovered

Creditors, trustees, or court officials might notice inconsistencies between the debtor's statements and the documentation provided, or they may receive tips from individuals who know of the debtor's actual financial situation. Advances in technology also make it easier to uncover financial transactions and holdings that debtors may be attempting to hide.

Investigation and Prosecution

If lies are discovered, the case may be referred to the U.S. Trustee's Office or the FBI for further investigation. If they find substantial evidence of fraud or perjury, the U.S. Attorney's Office will prosecute the crime.

Being honest and transparent in all bankruptcy dealings is imperative. The consequences of lying are severe and not worth the risk of attempting to protect assets from creditors. Debtors should work closely with their bankruptcy attorney to ensure that all information disclosed in the bankruptcy process is accurate and complete.

18

Loan Fraud

Pre-Bankruptcy Loan Fraud

Before the bankruptcy, the borrower inflates the value of property used as collateral to obtain a loan. This can be considered loan fraud for several reasons:

• **False Statements**: By inflating the value of the collateral, the borrower is making false statements to the lender about the true worth of the property.

• **Intent to Deceive**: The borrower intentionally deceives the lender in order to secure a larger loan amount.

• **Reliance by Lender**: The lender relies on the fraudulent appraisal to make the loan, which they might not have done or might have done under different terms if the true value had been known.

Bankruptcy Fraud

During bankruptcy, the debtor then deflates the property's value with the aim of reducing the amount that must be repaid, which can lead to accusations of:

• **Concealment of Assets**: The debtor is effectively concealing the true value of the assets from the court and creditors.

• **False Statements/Oaths**: Bankruptcy proceedings require truthful disclosure under penalty of perjury. Providing false information about the value of assets can lead to perjury charges.

• **Bankruptcy Fraud**: This type of manipulation of asset values falls under the umbrella of bankruptcy fraud, as it is an attempt to manipulate the bankruptcy process to obtain an undeserved financial advantage.

Discovery and Investigation

The discrepancy in property valuation might be discovered by:

• **Creditors**: Creditors may independently appraise the property and challenge the valuation presented by the debtor.

• **Bankruptcy Trustee**: The trustee assigned to the case may notice irregularities in the valuation of assets compared to the amounts of the secured loans.

• **Audit**: A random or targeted audit by the bankruptcy court may reveal the fraudulent valuations.

The investigation would likely be carried out by the United States Trustee Program, which is part of the Department of Justice, and if necessary, referred to the Federal Bureau of Investigation (FBI).

Prosecution and Penalties

If found guilty of these crimes, the debtor could face:

• **Criminal Charges**: The U.S. Attorney's Office prosecutes federal crimes and would handle cases of bankruptcy and loan fraud.

• **Prison Time**: Convictions can lead to substantial prison sentences, with bankruptcy fraud carrying a potential sentence of up to five years in prison.

• **Fines**: Significant fines may be imposed, potentially exceeding the amount of the loan or the value of the property.

• **Restitution**: The court may order the debtor to repay the defrauded amount to the lender or creditors.

By engaging in these fraudulent activities, debtors not only risk severe legal penalties but also undermine the integrity of the bankruptcy system, which is designed to provide relief to honest individuals who are overwhelmed by debt.

PART IV

How to Win the Property War in Your Bankruptcy

19

The War In Bankruptcy

Now you have the background that we can meet on common ground and have our heart-to-heart talk. The purpose of the trustee in bankruptcy is to take all the property away from you that here she can, sell it, and give the proceeds to your creditors – – plus keeping a percent for himself. Your job and your lawyers job in bankruptcy is to tell all about the property you have and reveal it, but then keep as much of it as you can legally. This is done and a number of ways and it is the wise bankruptcy filer who knows these ways, before he approaches a lawyer to help him, and before he and the lawyer file his case in court.

You are at the beginning...

Navigating bankruptcy is akin to steering a ship through a storm. One of the most crucial aspects of this journey is managing and retaining your property. This chapter delves into strategies and insights that can help you emerge from bankruptcy with your most valued assets intact. Understanding your rights and options can make the difference between a fresh start and a prolonged struggle.

Understanding Bankruptcy and Property

Types of Bankruptcy: First, understand the types of bankruptcy - Chapter 7 (Liquidation) and Chapter 13 (Reorganization). Each type has different implications for your property.

Keeping Property in a Chapter 7

1. Reaffirmation.

2. Buy your property back from the trustee

Exemptions and Non-Exempt Assets: Learn about exemptions in your state. Bankruptcy law allows you to keep certain "exempt" property. Knowing what assets are protected can help you plan more effectively.

The Role of the Trustee: In a Chapter 7 case, a trustee is appointed to oversee your assets. Their role is to sell non-exempt property to pay your creditors. Understanding their function is key to protecting your interests.

Strategic Planning

Assessment of Assets: Take a thorough inventory of your assets. Knowing exactly what you own, and its value, is the first step in formulating a strategy.

Maximizing Exemptions: Utilize exemptions strategically. Consult with a bankruptcy attorney to explore how state and federal exemptions can be best applied to protect your most valuable assets.

Consider Chapter 13: For those with significant assets, Chapter 13 bankruptcy often offers a better route. It allows you to keep your property by reorganizing debt into a manageable repayment plan.

Navigating the Process

Accurate Disclosure: Always provide accurate and complete information about your assets. Hiding or undervaluing assets can lead to serious legal consequences.

Negotiations and Settlements: In some cases, you can negotiate with creditors or the trustee to retain certain assets. This might involve paying a lump sum or agreeing to a repayment plan.

Legal Representation: Consider hiring a bankruptcy attorney. Professional guidance can be invaluable in navigating the complex terrain of bankruptcy law and protecting your property.

Post-Bankruptcy Strategy

Rebuilding Credit: After bankruptcy, focus on rebuilding your credit. This is crucial for your financial future and the potential acquisition of new assets.

Asset Management: Develop a plan for managing and protecting your retained or newly acquired assets post-bankruptcy.

Long-Term Financial Planning: Bankruptcy should be a stepping stone to a more secure financial future. Engage in long-term financial planning to avoid future financial distress.

Conclusion

Winning the property war in bankruptcy requires careful planning, a deep understanding of bankruptcy law, and sometimes, professional legal assistance. By strategically managing your assets, maximizing your exemptions, and choosing the right type of bankruptcy, you can protect your property and pave the way for a brighter financial future. Remember, bankruptcy is not the end, but a new beginning.

20

Reaffirmation Agreement

Understanding Reaffirmation Agreements
What is Reaffirmation?

• In a Chapter 7 bankruptcy, a reaffirmation agreement is a legal contract between the debtor and a creditor that excludes a specific debt from the bankruptcy discharge. This means you agree to continue paying the debt as if the bankruptcy filing never occurred.

Secured Debts and Assets:

• Reaffirmation is typically used for secured debts. When you reaffirm a debt, you agree to continue making payments to keep the asset that secures the debt, such as a vehicle or home.

The Process of Reaffirmation
Agreement Initiation:

• The process usually begins when the creditor offers a reaffirmation agreement to the debtor. This may occur shortly after the filing of the bankruptcy.

Terms of the Agreement:

• The reaffirmation agreement will detail the amount owed, the repayment schedule, and the interest rate. It essentially reinstates the original terms of the loan or sometimes offers slightly modified terms.

Legal Review and Approval:

• Once an agreement is made, it must be approved by the bankruptcy court. This often involves a hearing where the court assesses whether the reaffirmation is in your best interest and whether you can afford the payments.

Voluntary Decision:

• Signing a reaffirmation agreement is voluntary. You're not required by law to reaffirm any debt, and you should carefully consider whether you can handle the continued payments.

Considerations and Consequences

Financial Impact:

• If you reaffirm a debt and then fail to make the payments, the creditor can repossess the collateral and sue you for any deficiency balance.

Credit Reporting:

• Reaffirmed debts continue to be reported to credit bureaus. Timely payments can have a positive impact on your credit score post-bankruptcy.

Legal Counsel:

• It's highly advisable to consult with a bankruptcy attorney before entering into a reaffirmation agreement. An attorney can help you understand the ramifications and negotiate the terms.

Alternatives to Reaffirmation:

• In some cases, you might have alternatives such as redeeming the property by paying its current value in a lump sum or simply surrendering the asset to discharge the debt.

Conclusion

Reaffirmation in Chapter 7 bankruptcy is a significant decision that can have long-lasting financial implications. It's essential to weigh the benefits of keeping the asset against the financial strain of continuing the debt payments. Always seek professional legal advice to understand fully how reaffirmation will affect your financial situation.

21

Valuation of Assets

When filing for bankruptcy, a debtor must provide an estimate of the value of their assets. This is a crucial step, as it can significantly impact the bankruptcy process, including the treatment of debts and the protection of assets. Here are strategic considerations a debtor should keep in mind when valuing assets for a bankruptcy petition:

Accurate and Realistic Valuation

Fair Market Value:

• Assets should be valued at their current fair market value, not what was paid for them or what they might be worth in the future. Fair market value is the price a willing buyer would pay and a willing seller would accept in an open and competitive market.

Professional Appraisals:

• For items with significant value, such as real estate or high-value personal property, it may be wise to obtain professional appraisals to ensure accuracy.

Avoid Undervaluing:

• Intentionally undervaluing assets can be seen as fraud and may lead to serious legal consequences, including the potential dismissal of the bankruptcy case or criminal charges.

Avoid Overvaluing:

• Overvaluing assets can be equally problematic. It may result in higher bankruptcy estate values, potentially leading to more of your assets being used to pay creditors, especially in a Chapter 7 bankruptcy.

Consideration of Exemptions

Exemption Planning:

• Different states have different exemption laws that allow debtors to keep certain property in bankruptcy. Knowing your state's exemptions can guide how you value your assets.

Maximize Exemptions:

• In some cases, it might be beneficial to use valuations that maximize the use of available exemptions, protecting as much property as possible from being seized by the bankruptcy trustee.

Consultation with a Bankruptcy Attorney

Legal Advice:

• A bankruptcy attorney can provide valuable advice on how to value your assets appropriately. They understand the nuances of bankruptcy law and can help navigate exemption planning.

Strategy Tailored to Your Case:

• Each bankruptcy case is unique. An attorney can help formulate a valuation strategy that considers your specific financial situation and the bankruptcy chapter you are filing under.

Documentation and Evidence

Keep Records:

• Maintain documentation for your valuations, including receipts, appraisals, or comparative market analysis for similar items.

Be Prepared to Defend Valuations:

• The bankruptcy trustee or creditors may challenge your valuations. Be prepared to provide evidence or reasoning for the figures you've provided.

Conclusion

Valuing assets in a bankruptcy petition requires a balance between accuracy and strategic exemption planning. It's essential to approach this process with honesty and thoroughness, keeping in mind the potential legal ramifications of misrepresentation. The guidance of a bankruptcy attorney can be invaluable in ensuring that your asset valuations are both legally compliant and strategically sound.

PART V

Chapter 11

Chapter 11 bankruptcy, commonly referred to as "reorganization" bankruptcy, is a legal process that allows businesses, including small businesses, to restructure their debts while continuing their operations. This article will delve into various aspects of Chapter 11 bankruptcy, particularly focusing on small businesses, and how it contrasts with larger corporate bankruptcies like that of Sears.

When and By Whom Chapter 11 Bankruptcies are Filed

Chapter 11 bankruptcies are typically filed by businesses that need time to restructure their debts but want to keep operating. Small businesses, defined as those with fewer debt obligations and a simpler operational structure, often resort to Chapter 11 when they face financial distress but have viable business models. This contrasts with large corporations, which may file for Chapter 11 due to more complex financial struggles and on a much larger scale.

Differences Between Small Business and Large Corporate Chapter 11 Bankruptcies

Complexity and Scale: The scale of the bankruptcy significantly differs. For example, in the Sears bankruptcy, the company dealt with billions in liabilities and complex corporate structures, whereas small business bankruptcies are generally less complex with smaller debt loads.

Cost and Duration: Small business bankruptcies are designed to be quicker and less expensive than those like Sears. They often bypass certain procedural requirements, allowing for a more streamlined process.

Oversight: The level of oversight and the involvement of creditors can differ. In large bankruptcies, there are often multiple creditors' committees, while in small business cases, there may be less formal creditor involvement.

The Chapter 11 Plan and Voting Process

The Chapter 11 plan is the cornerstone of the bankruptcy process. It outlines how the business will restructure its debts and operate moving forward. Creditors vote on the plan, and for it to be approved, it must receive the majority vote from the creditors holding two-thirds of the total debt in each class of claims. The plan must be fair and equitable and offer a better outcome than liquidation under Chapter 7.

Obtaining New Debt in Chapter 11

Businesses under Chapter 11 can obtain new debt, known as "debtor-in-possession" financing, which can be crucial for revitalizing operations. This new debt often has priority over existing debts and can provide the necessary liquidity for a business to continue operating and restructure successfully.

The Role of the Trustee in Chapter 11

In Chapter 11 cases, a trustee may be appointed to oversee the bankruptcy process, though this is less common in small business cases. The trustee's responsibilities include reviewing the debtor's financial operations, assisting in the formulation of a reorganization plan, and ensuring compliance with bankruptcy law.

Chapter 11 Bankruptcy Overview

Chapter 11 bankruptcy provides a lifeline for businesses struggling with debt but still possessing viable business models. It allows for the restructuring of debts and offers a chance to emerge stronger and more financially stable. While this process can be complex and challenging, it offers an alternative to liquidation and can preserve jobs, business relationships, and the business itself.

In conclusion, Chapter 11 bankruptcy, especially for small businesses, is a critical tool for managing financial distress and offers a path to recovery and continued operation. Its distinct features, compared to large-scale corporate bankruptcies, make it accessible and practical for small businesses facing financial challenges.

22

Chapter 11 Reorganization

PART VI

Hiding Assets

Chapter 23

24

Our Final Talk

Too many times to count I've had clients ask about hiding assets. I'm not talking about hiding your dirt bike in aunt Mary's garage. No, I'm talking much bigger than that, especially to the individuals who would like to take their assets and hide them offshore in foreign accounts. For those of you who are thinking this way, as you know, there are filing requirements for US citizens, keeping offshore accounts and the failure to file, in those situations can be extremely painful if you dislike prison. So, first rule: do not hide a property. Let me say it again: do not hide property. Let's look at what can happen if property is hidden.

Hiding assets during a bankruptcy proceeding is a serious offense and can lead to severe legal consequences. Bankruptcy fraud, which includes concealing assets to avoid their liquidation or to deceive creditors or the bankruptcy court, is a federal crime in the United States.

Potential Consequences of Hiding Assets in Bankruptcy:

Criminal Charges: Hiding assets can result in federal criminal charges. The individual may be charged with bankruptcy fraud, which is a federal crime.

Dismissal of Bankruptcy Case: The bankruptcy court can dismiss the debtor's case. This means the debtor would lose the protections of bankruptcy, such as the automatic stay against creditor actions and the ability to discharge debts.

Denial of Discharge: Even if the case is not dismissed, the court can deny the discharge of the debtor's debts, meaning the debtor remains liable for all debts, including those that would normally have been discharged in bankruptcy.

Fines and Penalties: Conviction of bankruptcy fraud can result in significant financial penalties. The debtor may be ordered to pay fines, which can be substantial.

Imprisonment: Bankruptcy fraud is punishable by imprisonment. The maximum sentence for each count of bankruptcy fraud is up to five years in prison.

Civil Lawsuits: Aside from criminal penalties, the debtor might also face civil lawsuits from creditors or the bankruptcy trustee.

Permanent Record: A conviction for bankruptcy fraud will result in a criminal record, which can have long-lasting impacts on the individual's life, including difficulties in finding employment, loss of professional licenses, and social stigma.

Duration of Imprisonment:

• The duration of imprisonment for bankruptcy fraud can vary depending on the severity of the offense, the amount of money involved, the debtor's criminal history, and other factors. Each count of bankruptcy fraud carries a maximum sentence of up to five years. However, the actual sentence will be determined based on the specific circumstances of the case and federal sentencing guidelines.

Conclusion:

Hiding assets in bankruptcy is a risky and illegal action that carries severe consequences, including the possibility of significant fines and imprisonment. Anyone considering or going through bankruptcy should be fully transparent and honest in their disclosures to avoid these potential legal ramifications. It's also advisable to seek legal counsel from a qualified bankruptcy attorney to navigate the process lawfully and effectively.

About the Author

John Ellsworth, Esq. is an author and practicing attorney. He has 47 full-length novels published and a long series of these information manuals for the lay person. His website is https://www.johnauthor lawyer.com/home. He also has a bookstore at https://www.jellsworth books.com. John's practice is limited to representation of authors and other artists, musicians, and folk artists. He also defends tax cases involving the public. These are usually audits and tax debt.